WHAT DO BUS DRIVERS DO ALL DAY?

By Emily Mahoney

SCHOOL BUS

EMERGENCY DOOR

Gareth Stevens
PUBLISHING

Please visit our website, www.garethstevens.com. For a free color catalog of all our high-quality books, call toll free 1-800-542-2595 or fax 1-877-542-2596.

Library of Congress Cataloging-in-Publication Data

Names: Mahoney, Emily Jankowski, author.
Title: What do bus drivers do all day? / Emily Mahoney.
Description: New York : Gareth Stevens Publishing, [2021] | Series: What do
    they do? | Includes bibliographical references and index. | Contents: An
    important job – Learning the routes – Inspecting the bus – Hitting
    the road – Special routes – End of the day – A busy day.
Identifiers: LCCN 2019045317 | ISBN 9781538256930 (library binding) | ISBN
    9781538256916 (paperback) | ISBN 9781538256923 (6 Pack) | ISBN 9781538256947 (ebook)
Subjects: LCSH: Bus drivers–Juvenile literature. | Bus driving–Juvenile
    literature. | CYAC: Bus drivers. | Bus driving.
Classification: LCC HD8039.M8 M45 2020 | DDC 388.3/22023–dc23
LC record available at https://lccn.loc.gov/2019045317

Published in 2021 by
Gareth Stevens Publishing
111 East 14th Street, Suite 349
New York, NY 10003

Copyright © 2021 Gareth Stevens Publishing

Editor: Emily Mahoney
Designer: Laura Bowen

Photo credits: Series art Dima Polies/Shutterstock.com; cover, p. 1 cate_89/Shutterstock.com;
pp. 5, 13 kali9/E+/Getty Images; p. 7 alejandrosoto/E+/
Getty Images; p. 9 Bob Noah/Shutterstock.com; p. 11 Stuart Monk/Shutterstock.com; p. 15
Syda Productions/Shutterstock.com; p. 17 Vadim Rodnev/Shutterstock.com;
p. 19 trezordia/Shutterstock.com; p. 21 kali9/iStock/Getty Images Plus/Getty Images.

Printed in the United States of America

Some of the images in this book illustrate individuals who are models. The depictions do not imply actual situations or events.

CPSIA compliance information: Batch #CS20GS: For further information contact Gareth Stevens, New York, New York, at 1-800-542-2595.

Find us on

CONTENTS

Boldface words appear in the glossary.

An Important Job

Being a bus driver is an important job! Getting people safely and **promptly** to where they need to go is a big **responsibility**. A bus driver must know how to drive a large bus. They must also know their **route** and greet people with a smile!

5

Learning the Route

A bus driver must first learn the route they will drive. Usually, a driver will spend some time learning the roads before they begin driving that route. School bus drivers practice their routes and learn their stops before the school year begins. Then they are ready for the first day of school!

7

Inspecting the Bus

To make sure that the bus is safe, the driver must **inspect** the bus. They check the windshield wipers, brakes, lights, and tires to see that they are working. They also check the weather so they can be prepared for any snow, rain, or wind.

Hitting the Road!

Once the bus has been inspected, it's time to get going! School bus drivers pick up their students. Bus drivers who work in the city pick up people at bus stops. They bring them to work or other places nearby! Drivers follow a **schedule** to make sure they are on time to their stops.

11

Bus drivers must pay attention to many things while they are driving. They must follow the road signs and watch what other drivers are doing. They must **monitor** traffic conditions and be cautious around road construction. They also need to make sure that their **passengers** are behaving, or acting the right way.

Once the passengers have reached their **destination**, it's on to the next route! The number of routes that a bus driver drives each day depends on the length of the route and how long it takes to drive it. Some drivers have different routes throughout the day. Others drive the same route many times.

Special Routes

A school bus driver might also drive special routes. They might drive students to a fun field trip. They might take the soccer team to their game at a different school after the school day is finished. Drivers prepare for these routes by looking at directions to see where they are going!

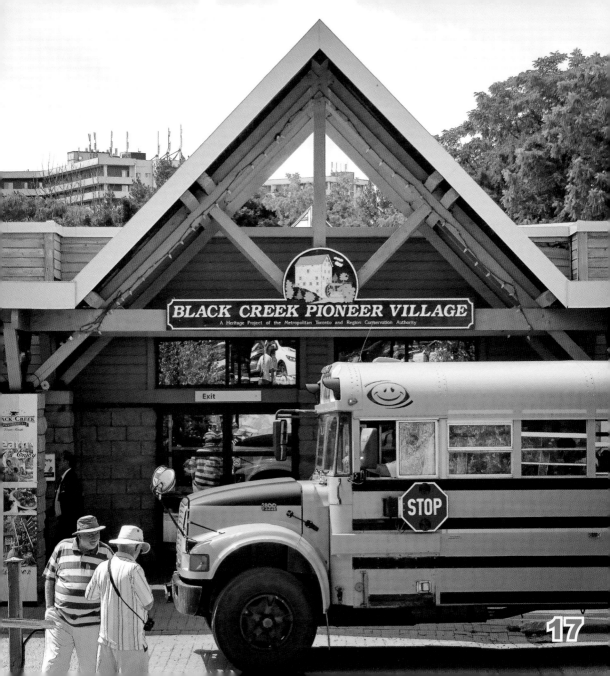

BLACK CREEK PIONEER VILLAGE

A Heritage Project of the Metropolitan Toronto and Region Conservation Authority

Exit

STOP

17

End of the Day

At the end of their route, there are a few things a bus driver must do before leaving. They clean their bus and fill it with gas for the next day. They close the windows if they were opened and complete any paperwork they need to do. Then they lock their bus to keep it safe overnight.

19

A Busy Day

Helping people to get where they need to go is a very important job, and a bus driver is an important job within a community. Whether they are driving a school bus or a city bus, every driver helps to keep their passengers safe and happy while they drive their route.

GLOSSARY

destination: the place to which somebody or something is going

inspect: to look over something carefully

monitor: to watch carefully

passenger: someone who rides on a plane, in a car, or on a bus

promptly: at the correct time

responsibility: something a person is in charge of

route: a course that people travel

schedule: a list of times when trains, planes, or buses will leave

FOR MORE INFORMATION

BOOKS

Park, Barbara. *Junie B. Jones and the Stupid Smelly Bus.* New York, NY: Random House, 2012.

Thomas, Penny M. *Nimoshom and His Bus.* Winnipeg, MB, Canada: HighWater Press, 2017.

WEBSITES

The Magic School Bus Games and Activities
scholastic.com/magicschoolbus/games/index.htm
This site has fun games and activities related to the Magic School Bus book series.

Staying Safe in the Car and on the Bus
kidshealth.org/en/kids/car-safety.html
Learn about how to be safe on a school bus from this website.

INDEX